SCIENCE
in Action

KEEPING HEALTHY

Why do I run?

Angela Royston

Quarto is the authority on a wide range of topics.

Quarto educates, entertains and enriches the lives of our readers—enthusiasts and lovers of hands-on living.

www.quartoknows.com

First published in the UK in 2016 by
QED Publishing
Part of The Quarto Group
The Old Brewery, 6 Blundell Street,
London, N7 9BH

A catalogue record for this book is available from the British Library.

ISBN 978 1 78493 628 0

Printed and bound in China

Publisher: Maxime Boucknooghe
Editorial Director: Victoria Garrard
Art Director: Miranda Snow
Design and Editorial: Starry Dog Books Ltd
Consultant: Dr Kristina Routh

Picture credits
(t=top, b=bottom, l=left, r=right, c=centre, fc=front cover)
Corbis Hutchings Stock Photography 12, Gareth Brown 16–17, Sam Diephuis/zefa 18, Emely/zefa 20.
Getty Images Kinson C Photography fc, Kaz Nanakubo 8, Tod Bigelow 13b, Erik Dreyer 16t.
Shutterstock Jacek Chabraszewski 4, Dragon Images 5tl, David Davis 5br, Sergei Kolesnikov 6, Losevsky Pavel 7b, Jeka 10, Gelpi 11t, phdpsx 11b, photobeps 13lt, cen 13lc, Dole 13lb, Matka Wariatka 14b, Sinan Isakovic 15, Serhiy Kyrychenko 17, (ball) Matt Antonino 18t, (pattern) Nataliya Hora 18t, Tamara Kulikova 19l, gorillaimages 19r, JJ pixs 21t.

Words in **bold** can be found in the glossary on page 22.

Contents

What is exercise?

Brain

Heart

Lungs

Hip bones

Leg muscles

When we exercise, our bodies work harder. This helps to keep us strong and healthy, and makes us feel good.

Running exercises our **muscles** and bones. It also makes our heart, lungs and brain work better.

4

Running is one type of exercise. Others include football, cycling, swimming, dance and gymnastics.

Walking is a great way to exercise. Walking to school is healthier than going by car.

Climbing and swinging are good exercise, and also great fun!

Strong muscles

Some of our muscles are attached to bones. We can move these muscles to make our bones move. The more we exercise, the stronger our muscles become.

This boy is using his arm muscles to move his arm bones.

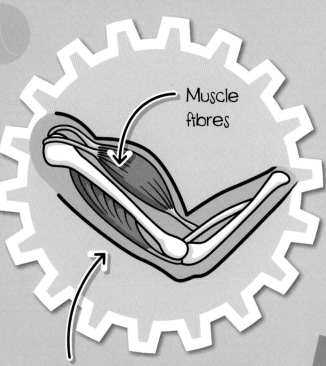

Muscle fibres

This big arm muscle is made of thick fibres.

Muscles are made of bundles of strings called fibres. When we exercise a muscle, the fibres get thicker and stronger. This makes the muscle bigger.

Activity

Feel your muscles. Sit on the floor with your legs bent in front of you. Hold the backs of your legs, then straighten your legs. Can you feel the muscles tightening?

7

Breathing

When we breathe, we take in **oxygen** from the air. Inside our bodies, the oxygen helps to release energy from the food we eat. When we exercise, our bodies need more energy, so we breathe faster to take in more oxygen.

Running makes us breathe faster.

Our lungs put oxygen into our blood.
Our heart then pumps the blood
around our bodies.

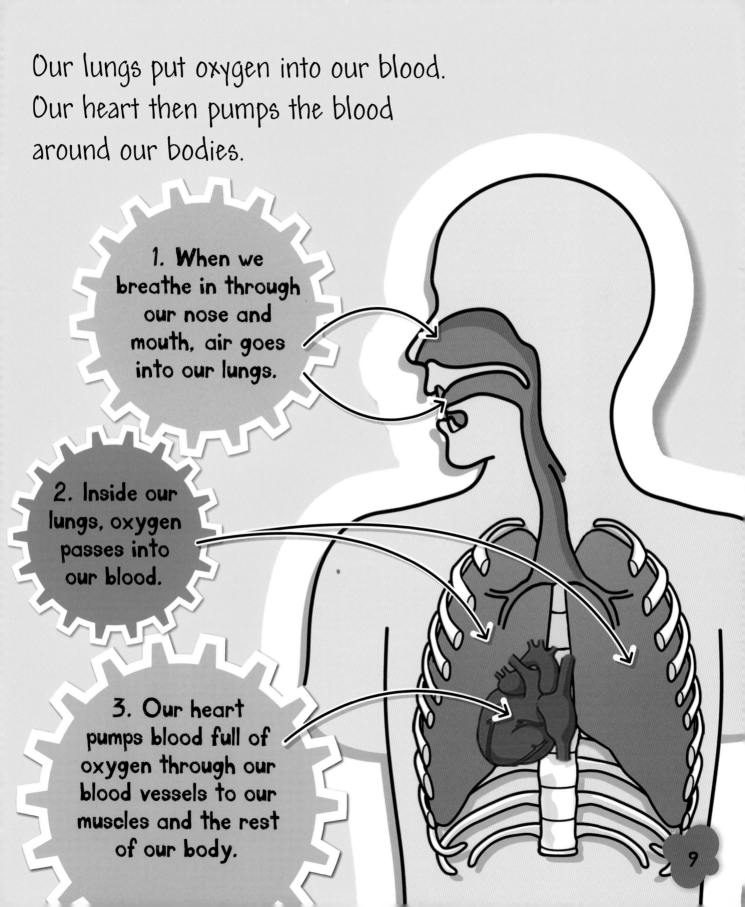

1. When we breathe in through our nose and mouth, air goes into our lungs.

2. Inside our lungs, oxygen passes into our blood.

3. Our heart pumps blood full of oxygen through our blood vessels to our muscles and the rest of our body.

9

Stamina

Exercise that makes us breathe faster helps our heart and lungs to work better. The better they work, the longer we can keep going. This is called having **stamina**.

This boy has lots of stamina. He can keep dancing without getting out of breath.

10

Activity

Stand still and breathe normally. Then run on the spot for two minutes. Notice how much harder you are breathing when you stop running.

Swimming is good exercise for the heart, which is a muscle.

Exercise that makes our hearts beat faster is called aerobic exercise. Running, swimming and dancing are all types of aerobic exercise. They make the heart stronger.

11

Strong bones

Our bones are strong. To help them stay strong, they use a substance called calcium. Some exercises help to make our bones stronger. For example, running and jumping puts extra force on our leg bones. This makes them take in more calcium.

Skipping makes our leg bones stronger.

Sardines

Cheese

Broccoli

Activity

Play a game such as cricket or baseball with a friend. Hitting a ball with a bat helps to make our arm bones stronger.

Sardines, cheese and broccoli contain calcium. Eating them helps to keep our bones strong.

Joints

Joints are the places where two bones meet, such as elbows and knees. We can only move our bones at our joints.

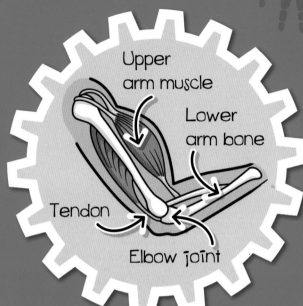

Upper arm muscle

Lower arm bone

Tendon

Elbow joint

Muscles are attached to bones by strong cords called **tendons**.

Activity

Stretch your hip joints. Sit on the floor and cross your legs. Take one foot and put it on the other knee. Can you do the same with the other foot?

Some types
of exercise stretch
our muscles and
tendons so that our
joints move more
easily. Ballet
dancing is a good
exercise for
stretching hip
and ankle joints.

Shoulder

Hip

Ankle

Ballet dancers
who practise a
lot have joints
that move easily.

Warming up

Before we do any energetic exercise, we need to warm up our muscles. We can do this by walking and then running gently.

Football players warm up their muscles by stretching.

These runners are stretching the tendons in their legs to warm up before a race.

Activity

Try these two warm-up exercises. Stand on one leg and bend the other foot back to touch your bottom. Next, stand with both legs straight. Bend over and, keeping both legs straight, touch one foot and then the other.

The more exercise we do, the fitter we become. But it's important to build up the amount of exercise we do gradually. A little bit more exercise each day makes our muscles stronger and increases our stamina.

17

Playing ball

In many sports, we need to throw and catch a ball. To do this well, we need good **co-ordination**. This means our eyes and hands need to work together so we time our movements correctly.

When we head a football, our brain, eyes and muscles must work together.

Co-ordination gets better with practice. You can practise by throwing a ball with friends or kicking a ball against a wall.

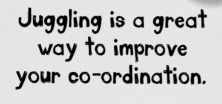

Juggling is a great way to improve your co-ordination.

Activity

Improve your ball skills! Keep a football in the air. You can use any part of your body except your hands and arms. How many 'keepie-uppies' can you do?

Cooling down

After doing energetic exercise, it's important that we slow down our heart and muscles gradually. To cool down after running, we could jog or walk for a few minutes.

After cooling down, rest for a while to let your body recover.

Exercise can make us hot and sweaty. If the air is cold, put on a jumper so that you don't cool down too fast.

Sweating often makes us thirsty, so it's good to drink after exercising.

Activity

Marching on the spot is a good cooling-down activity. March slower and slower, and then stop.

Glossary

Co-ordination
This is when eyes and muscles work together so we move at the right time. When we catch a ball, our eyes track the path of the ball and our muscles move our hands to catch it.

Joint
The place where two bones meet and fit together. Most joints allow the bones to move in a particular way, such as up and down.

Muscles
Parts of the body that we use to move. Some muscles move bones. Our tongue and heart are also muscles.

Oxygen
Oxygen is a gas found in air. Every part of our body needs oxygen to work properly. Our heart pumps blood full of oxygen all around the body.

Stamina
The ability to keep going when we are exercising. If we have plenty of stamina, our lungs can take in a lot of air without us having to breathe very fast, and our heart can pump a lot of blood around our bodies.

Tendon
A tough strap that attaches a muscle to a bone across a joint.

Index

NEXT STEPS

❊ Encourage children to keep themselves healthy. Talk to them about how exercise is good for their health because it makes their muscles and bones stronger, and makes their heart and lungs work better. Explain that exercise also makes people feel good.

❊ Children are most likely to exercise if they enjoy it. Health experts recommend that all children should exercise for at least an hour a day. This does not have to be all at once, and is often best broken down into periods of 15 minutes.

❊ Encourage children to walk or cycle to school with an adult, instead of going by car.

❊ Encourage children to exercise during breaks at school. They could play on the climbing frame or play ball games.

❊ Out of school, give children plenty of opportunities to take part in sports and activities they enjoy, such as football, swimming or dancing. Join in, too – most children enjoy practising football or throwing a Frisbee with an adult.

❊ Take children to a local park where they can have fun and keep healthy by playing on swings, roundabouts and other equipment.

❊ Children with heart or breathing problems must always be carefully supervised when they do exercise, and should not be allowed to over-exert themselves.